ᔕᔓ

Prayers for Help and Healing

ᔕᔓ

WILLIAM BARCLAY

Prayers for Help and Healing

HARPER & ROW, PUBLISHERS
New York, Evanston, San Francisco, London

PRAYERS FOR HELP AND HEALING. *Copyright © 1968 by William Barclay. Printed in the United States of America. All rights reserved. No part of this book may be used or reproduced in any manner whatsoever without written permission except in the case of brief quotations embodied in critical articles and reviews. For information address Harper & Row, Publishers, Inc., 10 East 53rd Street, New York, N.Y. 10022.*

FIRST HARPER & ROW PAPERBACK EDITION PUBLISHED IN 1975.

LIBRARY OF CONGRESS CATALOG CARD NUMBER: 68–29568

ISBN: 0-06-060481-6

Contents

∽∽

Foreword

The book is meant to be especially for those in illness, and particularly for those in hospital, and in infirmary, and in nursing homes, and for those in any kind of trouble. The general pattern is that there is first a prayer and then a verse of scripture and then the verse of a hymn.

This little book originated in the pages of *The British Weekly* although much has been added to it since the Prayers appeared there. The title and form of the book and, in fact, the whole idea of the book were not mine. The idea of the book originated in the mind of my very close friend, the Revd. Stanley C. Munro, M.A., Minister of Battlefield East Church in Glasgow. It was he who thought that such a book might be useful and it was he who suggested many of the titles of the Prayers and it was out of his pastoral concern for his own people and for other people that the idea of the book came. I am much indebted to him for providing me with the idea and the ideal of this book.

I hope that this little book may do something to bring peace and comfort to those who are going through any difficult time in body, mind or spirit.

William Barclay

University of Glasgow

Introduction
Christianity and Health

∽∾

In discussions about health there is a word which has become increasingly common. It is the word *psychosomatic*. *Psychosomatic* is compounded of two Greek words, *psychè*, which means the soul, and *sōma*, which means the body. So the word psychosomatic describes something which comes from, or affects, both soul and body at the same time. So nowadays it is commonly said that illness is psychosomatic. There was a time when illnesses were divided into two classes, those which affected the body and the causes of which were physical, and those which affected the mind or the spirit, and the causes of which were mental or spiritual. That distinction is less and less made nowadays. When a man is ill nowadays, it is not said that it is either his body or his mind that is ill. Rather the whole man is ill. We have come to see that it is not possible to make a clear division between body and soul, or body and mind, or body and spirit. The body and the mind or soul or spirit are so intertwined and interwoven and connected that nothing can happen to the one without affecting the other.

It is not difficult to see how this works. The mind can affect the body. We can, for instance, think ourselves into illness. If a man thinks he is ill, he will be ill. Nervous tension can literally raise the blood pressure or produce a stomach ulcer or open the way for the coming of a coronary thrombosis. I was recently talking to a well-known physician about the commonness of the coronary thrombosis. He was saying that at least one case of that trouble came into his hospital every day in the year. It so happened that two of my own friends had been stricken by this trouble very recently, and it so happens that neither of them has a spare ounce of flesh on him, neither of them smokes, one of them is a convinced and complete total abstainer, and the other is very moderate in his use of alcohol. I told this to the famous doctor. He

7

was silent for a moment. Then he said to me: 'I'm not a Christian. Sometimes I would call myself a humanist or even an atheist. But I do say this—if you want to avoid a thrombosis, never forget to say your prayers.'

What he meant was that the peace of mind, the freedom from tension, the relaxedness that trust and faith in God can bring are far and away the best defence that a man can have against illness. We have all seen this effect of the mind on the body in a very simple way. It often happens that when we have an engagement which we do not wish to face, when we have a task which we do not wish to do, when we know that in the course of the day we will have to face something of which we are really afraid, we often wake in the morning with a headache or with a streaming cold. It was the mind which produced the headache and the cold. That is not to say that they are any the less real and any the less serious. But this in effect was our mind seeking to provide us with an escape route from the thing that we did not wish to do.

The effect of the mind on the body is something which almost all of us have experienced. Call it the mind, the spirit, the soul, what you will, the link between it and the body is intimate and unbreakable. Paul Tournier in *A Doctor's Casebook in the Light of the Bible* quotes an example of just how close this connection is. 'There was, for example,' he writes, 'the girl whom one of my friends had been treating for several months for anaemia, without much success. As a last resort, my colleague decided to send her to the medical officer of the district in which she worked in order to get his permission to send her to a mountain sanatorium. A week later the patient brought word back from the medical officer. He proved to be a good fellow, and had granted the permit, but he added: "On analysing the blood, however, I do not arrive at anything like the same figures as those you quote." My friend, somewhat put out, at once took a fresh sample of blood, and rushed to his laboratory. Sure enough, the blood-count had suddenly changed. "If I had not been the kind of person who keeps carefully to laboratory routine," my friend went on, "and if I had not previously checked my figures at each of my patient's visits, I might have thought that I had made a mistake." He returned to his patient and asked her: "Has anything out of the ordinary happened in your life since your last visit?" "Yes, something has happened," she answered. "I have suddenly been able to forgive someone against whom I bore a nasty grudge; and all at once I felt as if I could at last say Yes to life!" ' The end of the bitterness of heart was the beginning of the cure of the illness. It may well be that we ought to examine our-selves to see if we are not at least to some extent responsible for our own troubles, for a person with a chip on his shoulder, a resentment against a person, or a grudge against life may well be a person whose illness will yield, not to a change of drugs or treatment, but to a change of heart. An unfor-giving person is necessarily an unhealthy person; a discon-tented person is on the way to being a sick person; an embittered person is already ill in mind and will end by being ill in body too.

If it is true that the mind can affect the body, it is equally true that the body can affect the mind and the spirit. The great masters of the spiritual life have seen that not infre-quently depression and spiritual gloom and dryness come from physical and not spiritual causes. Paul Tournier writes: 'The body is like a dog; if it is treated as an enemy, it snarls.' Philip Doddridge (1702-1751) wrote a once famous book entitled *The Rise and Progress of Religion in the Soul*, in which amongst other things he discussed these times of spiritual dryness, when a man feels that God is 'hiding his face' from him. In it he urges a man who is passing through one of these times to make certain that the cause of it is not physical rather than spiritual. 'And here,' he writes, 'I would first advise you most carefully to enquire, Whether your present distress does indeed arise from causes which are truly spiritual? Or whether it rather may not have its foundation in some disorder of body or in the circumstances of life in which you are providentially placed, which may break your spirits and deject your mind? . . . The state of the blood is often such as necessarily to suggest gloomy ideas even in dreams and to indispose the soul for taking pleasure in anything: and, when it is so, why should it be imagined to proceed from any peculiar divine displeasure, if it does not find its usual delight in religion? . . . When this is the case,

9

the help of the physician is to be sought rather than that of the divine, or, at least, by all means together with it; and medicine, diet, exercise, and air may in a few weeks effect that which the strongest reasonings, the most pathetic exhortation or consolations, might for many months have attempted in vain.' Still more famous as a spiritual director was Richard Baxter (1615-1691), author of the famous spiritual classic *The Saints' Everlasting Rest.* He makes exactly the same point. ' I advise thee,' he writes, ' as a further help to this heavenly life, not to neglect the due care of thy bodily health. Thy body is an useful servant if thou give it its due and no more than its due; but it is a most devouring tyrant if thou suffer it to have what it unreasonably desires; and it is as a blunted knife if thou unjustly deny it what is necessary to its support.' He goes on to warn against giving the passions of the body free rein. But after that warning he goes on to say: ' There are a few who much hinder their heavenly joy by denying the body its necessaries, and so making it unable to serve them; if such wronged their flesh only, it would be no great matter; but they wrong their soul also; as he that spoils the house injures the inhabitants. When the body is sick, and the spirits languish, how heavily do we move in the thoughts and joys of heaven!'

The great masters of the spiritual life have seen that the best way to injure the spiritual life is to neglect the body. We may well be warned to have a care that when we are spiritually depressed the road we ought to take is to the doctor's surgery rather than to the Church in the first place. An ailing and inefficient body can go far to produce a depressed mind and spirit.

To set this importance on the body is thoroughly Christian. It has been one of the mistakes of religious thought that far too often the body has been suspect, and even feared and despised. This has been so for two reasons. The first reason is quite simply the troubles that the body can bring. It is vulnerable to pain and disease and distress. As the years go on, it develops its own weaknesses and its own slow but inevitable breakdown. If its passions and its desires are uncontrolled, it can bring troubles for itself and for others. Experience teaches both the weakness and the dangers of the body, and it was not unnatural that it was blamed for the ills to which human life is heir.

The second reason is much more far-reaching, and has left a deep mark on men's attitude to the body. When Christianity came into the world there was a type of thought called Gnosticism. Gnosticism, like many another system, tried to explain the source and origin of sin and evil and pain and suffering. It did so by means of a thoroughgoing dualism. Its belief was that from the beginning there were two entities, spirit and matter. Matter is eternal; it has been there from the beginning; and it was, so they believed, the raw material of creation. But the Gnostic believed that from the beginning this matter was flawed and bad and imperfect. Out of this bad stuff everything that was made was created. Since this raw material was bad, it could never be touched or handled or used by the true God, who in his perfection could never touch that which was imperfect. The creator God, the Demiurge they called him, is therefore not the same as the true God. He is an inferior God, ignorant of and indeed hostile to, the true God. It therefore follows that all that has ever been created is bad and evil. All creation was made out of bad stuff by an ignorant God. All creation is evil. Therefore, the body is evil. It can never be cured, tamed, reformed. It is essentially and incurably and unchangeably evil. So Epictetus can speak of himself as a poor soul shackled to a corpse. Seneca can speak of the detestable habitation of the body. Plato can describe the body as the prison-house of the soul. This line of thought was very prevalent in the early days of Christianity. It even, perhaps unconsciously, permeated Christian thought. And so there came the idea that the body as such is an evil thing, and it is only the soul, the spirit which matters.

The Christian view of the body is very different from that. So far from being something which is essentially evil, for the Christian the body is something which can be offered to God as a sacrifice. 'I appeal to you, therefore,' writes Paul to the Romans, ' by the mercies of Christ to present your bodies as a living sacrifice, holy and acceptable to God, which is your spiritual worship' (Romans 12.1). The body—and to this we will return—can be nothing less than the temple of the

11

Holy Spirit, and is meant for the Lord (I Corinthians 6.13, 19; cp.3.16). This is what the New Testament thinks of the body. Apart from anything else, if we believe in the incarnation, we believe that in Jesus God, as it were, took a human body upon himself. The eternal Word became for a time a flesh and blood person with a body (John 1.14). Surely we can never despise or regard with contempt that which God took upon himself. To the Christian the body matters, because God took it upon himself, and because it can be offered to God.

The deliberate hatred and neglect of the body reached its peak in the monks and the hermits of the fourth century. They retired to the desert to live in communities or absolutely alone. To them a filthy, unkempt body was a virtue. They gloried in never washing or taking a bath, and they were accounted as specially holy because ' lice dropped from them as they walked '. They deliberately starved themselves so that they became thin and emaciated. Everything was done to show their contempt of the body. They often used—or rather misused—the saying of Paul. ' I pommel my body and subject it,' Paul said (I Corinthians 9.26). But we have only to read the whole passage in which that saying occurs to see that what Paul is speaking about is the disciplined training of the athlete, in which he trains his body to make it fitter for strenuous effort, not the asceticism of the ascetic, who has no object beyond asceticism for its own sake. By all means, discipline for greater fitness; by no means, asceticism for its own sake.

Discipline for fitness brings us to two great reasons why the body and its health are important.

First, the health of the body is important because the body is the instrument and agent of the mind. The mind thinks and plans. Its thoughts and its plans have to be put into operation, and the body has a large part to play in the actualising and the realising of the ideas and the ideals of the mind. It is a frustrating experience to find that the mind's plan cannot be put into operation because the body has been allowed to become flabby and unfit. The body is the servant of the mind, and to be guilty of slackness and carelessness and indiscipline in the use of it is no small error.

Second, the body is more than that. The body is the instrument of God, because the body is the temple of the Holy Spirit (I Corinthians 6.19). It is through us that God's purposes have to be realised, and it is our duty to keep ourselves fit to be the instruments of God. There is a wonderful text in the Old Testament. There was a time when the Midianites were making things intolerably difficult for the Israelites. God sought for a champion to deliver his people, and found that champion in Gideon. Then there comes the sentence: 'The Spirit of the Lord took possession of Gideon' (Judges 6.34). The literal translation of the Hebrew is: 'The Spirit of the Lord clothed himself with Gideon.' It is as if to say that the Spirit used Gideon as a body to win freedom for his people. We have, in so far as we can make it so and keep it so, to make our body fit to be used for the purposes of God.

From all this two things emerge, and they ought to be clearly stated, for they are often misunderstood. The first is the basic truth that no illness, no pain and no suffering are the will of God. There are people who will say of any illness and of any suffering or accident, and even of any tragic happening: 'Well, it's God's will.' There are those who will go into the house of pain or mourning and talk about it all as the will of God. Suffering and disease and pain are in fact contrary to the will of God, and it is the purpose and the plan of God that the time should come when these things will no longer be, precisely because in that future time the will of God will be perfectly realised.

The evidence in Scripture for this is overwhelming. It is the dream of the prophet in the Old Testament that there will come a time when no one will say: 'I am sick' (Isaiah 33.24). From the beginning to the end of the ministry of Jesus healing is an integral part of his work (Mark 1.39; Matthew 9.35; Luke 6.17). When the disciples of John the Baptist asked whether he was the One who was to come or if they must go on waiting and hoping for someone else, it was to his ministry of healing that Jesus pointed as the evidence for who he was (Matthew 11.5; Luke 7.22). He said that his healing work was the very proof that the Kingdom had come (Matthew 12.28; Luke 11.20). When he sent out his disciples, they were not only to teach and preach; they were also to heal (Matthew 10.8; Luke 9.2). The defeat of disease was one of the greatest features of Jesus' ministry and one of the marks of the emergence of the Kingdom of God.

Illness and pain and disease are never the will of God. They are always the proof that something has gone wrong which God wishes to put right.

The second truth which emerges from all this is that the doctor is the servant and the helper of God. Paul Tournier points out that there are still people who have what might be called a suspicion of medicine. He cites the case of a woman hernia patient whom he was treating. He advised her to consult a surgeon. She refused. ' I don't want ', she said, ' to depend on anyone but Jesus Christ.' He tells of a patient whom he was treating in collaboration with a psychiatrist, who had prescribed a sleeping-draught to be taken every night. ' I take it,' the man told Tournier, ' and it does me good. I am more relaxed, less nervous, and I work better; and yet I must confess that I never take it without a twinge of conscience. It is as if to use an artificial method were a sign of lack of faith in God.' ' But ', Tournier answered, ' that medicine is also a blessing from God, just like the bread he gives us every day!' ' To have recourse to the doctor's skill, or to eat the baker's bread, these are one and the same thing.'

No one need ever feel that to use the methods and the skills of medicine as advised and prescribed by a wise doctor is in any sense a sign of lack of faith. It is simply to use the gifts which God has mercifully given to us.

It is also, as we have already said, to say that the doctor is the helper of God. Paul Tournier quotes some great sayings about this relationship of the doctor with God. Professor Courvoisier wrote that the vocation of medicine is ' a service to which those are called who through their studies and the natural gifts with which the Creator has endowed them . . . are especially fitted to tend the sick and to heal them. Whether or not they are aware of it, whether or not they are believers, this is from the Christian point of view fundamental, that doctors are, by their profession, fellow workers with God.' ' The doctor,' wrote Alain Perrot, ' is an instrument of God's patience.' ' Medicine is a dispensation of the grace of God, who in his goodness takes pity on men and provides remedies for the evil consequences of sin,' wrote Dr. Schlemmer. John Calvin declared that medicine is a gift from God. 'Thus,' concludes Tournier, 'every doctor, Christian or not, is a collaborator with God.' Medical and surgical treatments are not an infringement of the rights of God; they are the use of the gifts of God.

This inevitably raises the question of what is called spiritual healing. There is a sense in which all healing is spiritual, because there is a real sense in which all healing is the action of God. Paul Tournier quotes the famous words of Ambroise Paré: 'I tended him. God healed him.' He then goes on to quote another incident in the life of Paré in which there is expressed 'this marriage of intellect and faith, technology and prayer.' 'The Marquis d'Auret,' wrote Paré, 'had a bullet wound in the joint of his knee and seemed at death's door . . . Howbeit, to give him courage and a good hope, I told him that I would soon set him on his feet . . . When I had seen him, I went for a walk in a garden, where I prayed God that he would grant me this grace, that the Marquis be healed, and that he would bless our hands, and the physics that were needed to fight so many complicated maladies . . I discoursed in my mind on the means I must adopt to do this.' Here is a doctor equally dependent on science and on God.

But spiritual healing in the narrower sense of the term is usually taken to mean the healing of disease by prayer and the laying on of hands, apart from the use of normal medical and surgical techniques. This is a subject on which no wise or careful person is going to speak dogmatically. But there are certain things to be said. What we say is to be taken as no more than one man's experience and opinion.

In the first place, it is extraordinarily difficult to track down a case of spiritual healing of a normal disease which is fully authenticated under medical controls and tests, and which is permanent. In the second place, the results of the practice of spiritual healing are, it would seem, completely unpredictable and erratic. If it is effective, it is effective in one case and not in another, and there seems to be no explicable reason for the difference. This erratic effect does produce very great difficulties for faith and belief. In the third place, it would seem more reasonable to use the normal gifts of healing which God has entrusted to us than to resort to the abnormal. It is not God's way to deal in gratuitous miracles, or to do for men what he has by his grace enabled them to do for themselves.

But, having said all that, we are quite certain that there is a place for the work of spiritual healing. But that place is not, we believe, as a substitute for normal healing, but as a collaborator and co-worker with it. One thing is quite certain —a man's mental and spiritual condition will have the very greatest effect on the healing of his illness. If he is tensed, nervous, worried, afraid, pessimistic, despairing, without the will to recover, and even without the faith and the hope that he will recover, then the work of the doctor and the surgeon will be made very much harder, and may indeed be frustrated altogether. What we do believe is that the techniques of spiritual healing, prayer, the laying on of hands, anointing and the like, can beget in a man an attitude and condition of mind and heart which will greatly advance the man's prospect of being healed and the speed of his recovery. We believe that spiritual healing can be the very greatest ally of what we might call natural healing. When the techniques of the physician and the surgeon meet the peace of faith in the patient, things become possible which would otherwise be impossible. This is not to deny that things happen which are beyond our understanding, but it is to say that the great contribution of spiritual healing will be made in co-operation with the physician and the surgeon, and not in separation from him.

This co-operation between the minister and the doctor, between the priest and the physician, will be specially valuable and effective in nervous troubles. One of the features of the age in which we live is the effect that the speed and the stress and the tension of living have had on people's minds and nerves. The nervous and the mental breakdown are characteristic troubles of our generation. Most often the root cause of these troubles is fear. There is the feeling that the universe is a hostile and a frightening place and that life is a terrifying experience with which the victim cannot cope. The basic cause of this is that the person involved is trying

16

to live life alone. John Buchan described an atheist as 'a man with no invisible means of support' To have to meet life with nothing more than we can bring to it is bound to be an experience which brings fear and defeat. In such a case the cure is to become certain that we meet nothing alone, but that we meet everything with God which is the way to be rid of fear and to live with confidence. In such cases the real cure is to learn to pray and to learn to know God as love.

Until now we have been thinking in terms of healing, but what of the times when there seems to be only pain and when there is humanly speaking no healing to be found? Even out of a situation like that great things can come. When Leighton, the Scottish divine, was in all his pain, he said: 'I have learned more of God since I came to this bed than ever I did before.' It is then that so many have found it true that in all their afflictions he was afflicted (Isaiah 63.9), and that when they passed through the waters God was with them (Isaiah 43.2). In that Jesus Christ himself was tested and tried, he can help others who are going through it (Hebrews 2.18)

My father had a story he loved to tell. There was a girl near where we used to live who was suffering from an incurable disease and who was slowly and painfully dying. He used from time to time to visit her. On one occasion he took with him a very lovely little book of comfort for those in trouble written by an anonymous author. He gave it to her. 'I thought,' he said, 'you might like to see it, and that it might help you.' 'I know this book,' she said. 'Have you got it already?' my father asked. She smiled and answered quietly: 'I wrote it.' Out of the furnace of affliction there had come, not only peace for herself, but also the power to help others. Even in the sorest day and even when all earthly help is gone the Christian can still say: 'I am sure that neither death, nor life, nor angels, nor principalities, nor things present, nor things to come, nor powers, nor height, nor depth, nor anything else in all creation, will be able to separate us from the love of God in Christ Jesus our Lord' (Romans 8.38, 39).

17

Prayers for Help and Healing

✍ Before going to the doctor ✍

O God,
I can no longer pretend to myself
  that everything will be all right
  if I just leave things alone.
I can no longer avoid the fact
  that there is something wrong.
Go with me when I go to my doctor today,
  and give me courage to face the truth about myself.
Make me quite sure that, whatever the verdict,
  I can face it with you.

Let me remember the promise of God:
When you pass through the waters I will be with you.

Isaiah 43.2

My times are in thy hand:
Why should I doubt or fear?
My Father's hand will never cause
His child a needless tear.

O God, my Father,
Now that I know that I must go into hospital,
   help me not to worry.
Help me to realise
   that worry only makes things worse,
   and that the more I worry
   the longer I will take to get better.
Teach me that I am just as near you
   in a hospital bed as in my own home.
Give me that peace of mind
   without which I know that I can't have health of body.

Let me learn what Paul learned:
   I have learned, in whatever state I am, to be content.
Philippians 4.11

Give to the winds thy fears;
Hope, and be undismayed;
God hears thy sighs and counts thy tears,
God shall lift up thy head.

O God,
Everything is new and strange and rather frightening.
Half the time I don't know what is going on.
Help me
   to be serene and calm and relaxed.
Keep me cheerful,
   and help me to be a comrade
   to those who are feeling
   just as strange and just as afraid as I am.
Help me
   not to grumble or complain.
Help me
   not to be fussy and demanding.
Help me
   to be grateful for all that is done for me.
Help me
   to make the work of those who are looking after
      me as easy as I can.
Help me
   to forget my own troubles
      in doing something to help and cheer
      those who are worse off than I am.

Help me to be as sure of God as the Psalmist was when he said:
God is our refuge and strength,
a very present help in trouble.   *Psalm 46.1*

   Hold thou my hands!
In grief and joy, in hope and fear,
Lord, let me feel that thou art near;
   Hold thou my hands!

O God,
   Help me to remember at this moment
   that I have a very great deal to be thankful for.
I am grateful
   for the wisdom of the physician,
   and the skill of the surgeon,
   and the art of the anaesthetist,
   and the kindness of the nurses.
I am grateful for the merciful oblivion
   which anaesthetics bring.
Help me
   to be calm and relaxed,
   trusting the surgeon,
   and the skill you gave him,
   and trusting you.
And make me quite sure
   that, whatever happens,
Nothing can separate me
   from your love in Christ Jesus, my Lord.

Let me pray Jesus' own prayer:
Father, into thy hands I commit my spirit!   *Luke 23.46*

Tell me thou art mine, O Saviour,
Grant me an assurance clear;
Banish all my dark misgivings,
Still my doubting, calm my fear.

O God,
Operations are all in the day's work
  for the surgeon and the doctor,
  and the anaesthetist and the nurse,
but for people like me
  they are strange and alarming.
I am so glad
  that I am through my operation,
  and that I am still alive!
I can say that to you,
  knowing that you will understand.
I know that this is only the first step
  on the way back to health.
Help me from now on
  to be a good patient,
  thankful and uncomplaining,
  always helping, never hindering
  those who are trying to make me well.

Let me remember the confidence of the Psalmist:
Why are you cast down, O my soul,
  and why are you disquieted within me?
Hope in God; for I shall again praise him,
  my help and my God.

Psalm 43.5

God merciful and righteous is,
  yea, gracious is our Lord,
God saves the meek; I was brought low,
  he did me help afford.

O God,
  My body won't act
  and my mind won't think,
  and I feel that I can't do anything.
  I'm too tired even to sleep.
The worst of it is that I feel
  that I will never be able to do anything again.
I get so utterly depressed.
  I've almost stopped hoping
  that I'll ever be fit again;
  and it doesn't seem worth while even trying.
Nothing seems to do any good,
  and there seems nothing left to do
  but to give up and to give in.
O God,
  Lighten my darkness;
  Strengthen my weakness;
  Put hope into my hopelessness.
  I'm beaten, unless you help me.
  Help me to believe that you will,
  Hear this my prayer through Jesus Christ our Lord.

Let me remember the experience of the Psalmist:
  I waited patiently for the Lord:
  He inclined to me and heard my cry.
  He put a new song in my mouth,
  A song of praise to our God.   *Psalm 40.1,3*

The secret of living:
To feel that though I journey on
By stony paths and rugged ways,
Thy blessed feet have gone before
And strength is given for weary days.

O God,
I just can't sleep.
I just can't stop thinking.
I just can't stop being afraid of the future.
I can't cope with things any longer,
   and I have got to a stage
   when I can't even rest.
I know that in the long run
   pills and drugs and sedatives
   are not really a cure.
Put your rest in my mind
   and your peace in my heart,
   that I may lean back
   and rest in you.

Let me take the advice of the Psalmist:
   Cast your burden on the Lord,
   and he will sustain you.

Psalm 55.22

When in the night I sleepless lie,
My soul with heavenly thoughts supply;
Let no ill dreams disturb my rest,
No powers of darkness me molest.

O God,
I've reached the stage
  when I just can't cope any longer,
  and it had to be this hospital for me.
I am so utterly tired
    and I can't concentrate.
My mind is so weary
  that I can't keep it on anything,
  and I can't control my thoughts.
The smallest task sets me worrying;
  things are always on the top of me.
The least thing irritates me,
  and I fly into a temper.
I get so depressed
  that I cry and can't stop crying.
I'm afraid of everything,
  afraid to meet people,
  afraid to go out,
  afraid to take a decision,
  afraid even to cross the street.
I just can't stop worrying.
I know that a mind is worse to cure than a body.
Help me to help myself
  by doing everything I can
  to co-operate with those who are trying to help me.
And, more than anything else,
  give me the peace of mind
  which comes from thinking
  not of myself but of you.

I remember that Jesus said: Why are you afraid? Why have
you no faith? Let me remember that he also said: Peace! Be
still!   *Mark 4.39,40*

'Tis only in thee hiding
I feel myself secure;
Only in thee abiding,
The conflict can endure.

Thine arm the victory gaineth
O'er every hateful foe;
Thy love my heart sustaineth
In all its cares and woe.

O God,
    Somehow things have gone all wrong.
I am always tired,
    and because I am tired
I am irritable,
    and because I am irritable
    there is always trouble between me
    and the people I live with.
I am always conscious of my body.
I have almost forgotten what it is like
    to feel fit and full of energy and life.
I have got to drive myself
    to do the work that used to be a pleasure.
I have got to toil at things
    that I used to do easily.
I used to be on top of my work,
    now it's on the top of me.
I used to enjoy life,
    but now life is a weariness.
O God,
    in hospital help me to find new strength
    and new zest for life.
Make me a good patient,
    so that I may help those
    who are doing their best to help me.

Let me remember that God's Spirit is on God's messenger
to give to all sufferers a garland instead of ashes,
the oil of gladness instead of mourning,
the mantle of praise instead of a faint spirit. *Isaiah 61.3*

Thy promise is my only plea,
With this I venture nigh;
Thou callest burdened souls to thee,
And such, O Lord, am I!

O God,
Sometimes I lie here and worry.
I worry
    about what is going to happen to myself,
    about what is going to happen to my work and to my job,
    and to those who are depending on me.
I worry
    about what is going to happen to the house and home,
    and about what is happening to the family
    with me not there.
After all, it would hardly be natural
    if I didn't.
I fear the worst,
    and sometimes I wonder
    if I am ever going to be well and strong again.
Give me
    the peace of mind
    which comes
    from leaving things to you.
Help me
    to feel the clasp of the everlasting arms
    underneath and about me,
    and to know
    that neither I nor those I love
    can ever drift
    beyond your love and care.

Let me remember the promise of Jesus:
    Peace I leave with you; my peace I give to you;
    not as the world gives do I give to you. Let not
    your hearts be troubled, neither let them be afraid.
                                                    John 14.27

I know not what the future hath
Of marvel or surprise,
Assured alone that life and death
His mercy underlies.

O God,
It is better to speak frankly about things
   than to bottle them up.
I can't help wondering
   why this should have happened to me.
I can't help feeling bitter and resentful.
I know that I shouldn't feel that way,
And I don't really want to feel that way.
I can't help feeling angry
   when people who have never known any trouble
   come and tell me
   that it is all for the best.
Whatever happens, keep me
   from querulous self-pity.
At least teach me
   that I have got to accept things,
   whether I like it or not,
   and bring me in the end
   to that faith
   which can accept even what it cannot understand.

Let me remember Moses' song:
   The eternal God is your dwelling-place,
   and underneath are the everlasting arms.
                              Deuteronomy 33.27

When we in darkness walk,
Nor feel the heavenly flame,
Then is the time to trust our God
And rest upon his name.

Lord Jesus,
You know what pain is like.
You know
   the torture of the scourge upon your back,
   the sting of the thorns upon your brow,
   the agony of the nails in your hands.
You know what I'm going through just now.
Help me
   to bear my pain
   gallantly, cheerfully and patiently,
And help me to remember
   that I will never be tried
   above what I am able to bear,
   and that you are with me,
   even in this valley of the deep dark shadow.

Let me remember what Paul said:
   God is faithful, and he will not let you be
   tested beyond your strength.   *I Corinthians* 10.13

In ev'ry pang that rends the heart,
The Man of Sorrows had a part;
He sympathises with our grief,
And to the suff'rer sends relief.

O God,
    When you've got a worried mind
    and a body you can't forget,
        it's not easy to sleep,
    and the trouble is,
        the more you try to sleep.
          the less you can sleep.
Thank you
    for those who watch all night
    to care for me,
        and for people like me.
Thank you
    for books to read
        when I can't sleep.
O God,
    stop my thoughts
        going round and round;
    stop my body
        being all tensed and strained.
If I must think,
    help me to think of your love,
    and of Jesus here with me all the time,
        so that, even if I can't sleep,
        I will be at peace.

Let me think about what the Psalmist said:
    Even the darkness is not dark to thee,
        the night is bright as the day;
        for darkness is as light with thee.   *Psalm 139.12*

Thee, in the watches of the night,
When I remember on my bed,
Thy presence makes the darkness light;
Thy guardian wings are round my head.

O God,
I can't help lying here
  and thinking about home.
I can't relax here
  the way I can relax at home,
    because everything is so strange.
I keep wondering
  how they are getting on without me,
and if they are worrying about me
  as much as I am worrying about them.
I wouldn't be human
  if I didn't miss my own home
    and my own people.
But help me to be sensible and to realise
  that the more I worry,
  and the more discontented I am,
    the slower will be my cure,
      and the longer I will be getting back to them.
And help me to remember
  that there are other people in this ward
    who are home-sick too.
So help me to forget my own loneliness
  in doing something which will help them
    to forget theirs.

Let me remember and let me echo Paul's great claim:
  I have learned, in whatever state I am, to be content.

Philippians 4.11

My times are in thy hand;
My God I wish them there;
My life, my friends, my soul I leave
Entirely to thy care.

O God,
I think that just about the worst thing about this
  is being separated from my family and my home.
Keep my husband/wife from worrying too much about me,
And keep the children from missing me too much.
Help me to realise
  that things will go on,
  even if I am not there,
And that it is not for all that long anyway.
Thank you
  for giving me good neighbours, good friends, good
    relations,
  to look after things and to help,
  when I am not there.
Help me to remember
  that the more I worry about them,
    the slower will be my recovery
      and the longer I will take to get back to them,
And help me
  to lie back and to relax
  for as long as I need,
  in the certainty that
  although I am separated from them
  you are still with them and me.

Let me remember the word of Jesus:
  They shall never perish, and no one shall
  snatch them out of my hand.   *John 10.28*

Guard them from every harm
When dangers shall assail,
And teach them that thy power
Can never, never fail;
We cannot with our loved ones be,
But trust them, Father, unto thee.

O God,
I have no one of my own at all now,
There isn't anyone to think about me
   or to worry about me.
I have friends and acquaintances,
   but I have no one at home
   of my own flesh and blood.
I'm not worried about being looked after.
I know that that will be done all right.
   But I can't help feeling lonely,
   and I can't help envying others
   who have people who really care for them.
Help me to remember that
   I have you as my Father,
And that I have Jesus
   as the Brother born to help
   in time of trouble.
And so help me to lose my loneliness
   in your love.

I can say with the Psalmist:
   Whom have I in heaven but thee?
   And there is nothing upon earth that
   I desire beside thee.

Psalm 73.25

I've found a friend; O such a friend!
   He loved me ere I knew him;
He drew me with the cords of love,
   And thus he bound me to him;
And round my heart still closely twine
   These ties which nought can sever,
For I am his, and he is mine,
   For ever and for ever.

O God,
From this illness of mine I have learned one thing anyway—
   that you have got to lose a thing for a time
   in order to value it when you get it back.
I never really appreciated my home until now.
   It's lovely to be back home;
   it's lovely to see and touch
     the old familiar things,
   and to be again with the people I love.
Help me to avoid two things.
Help me to avoid
   trying to do too much
     in order to show how well I am,
   and so undoing all the good
     that has been done to me in hospital.
And help me to avoid
   acting the invalid,
     and expecting to be waited on hand and foot.
Give me a grateful heart
and a sensible mind,
   and help me to make steady progress,
     until I am a hundred per cent fit again.

Like the Psalmist I am glad because
God setteth the solitary in families.   *Psalm 68.6* AV

Help us, O Lord, our homes to make
Thy Holy Spirit's dwelling-place;
Our hands and heart's devotion take
To be the servants of thy grace.
Teach us to keep our homes so fair,
That were our Lord a child once more,
He might be glad our hearth to share,
And find a welcome at our door.

O God,
I think that everyone has done all that can be done,
   and I have the feeling
   that it is not enough.
So I'm coming to you now
   because I have nowhere else to go.
Make me quite sure that, whatever happens,
nothing can separate me from you,
that, whether I get better or not,
I am in your hands.
Help me,
   not to be afraid any more,
   and not to worry any more.
I'm not giving in:
I'll still hold on to life,
   and do everything to get well.
But make me sure that,
   whether I live or die,
you are with me always,
   to the end—and beyond the end.

Let me remember the faith of the Psalmist:
   In peace I will both lie down and sleep,
   for thou alone, O Lord, makest me dwell in safety.
                     Psalm 4.8

Abide with me; fast falls the eventide;
The darkness deepens; Lord with me abide:
When other helpers fail, and comforts flee,
Help of the helpless, O abide with me.

O God,
They don't need to tell me
　　that it is going to be touch and go with me.
I know quite well
　　that I've got to be ready for anything.
I know that the surgeons and the doctors and the nurses
　　will do their very best for me.
Give me the will to win through.
Give me
　　patience to bear my weakness,
　　courage to endure my pain,
　　obedience to accept whatever is best for me.
If I am not to get better,
　　make me quite sure that,
　　whether I live or die,
　　nothing can separate me from your love.
I think that I have got past the stage of worrying,
But I know how anxious those who love me are,
Bless them and help them not to worry,
　　but to leave everything to you;
　　because that is what I am doing.

Let me remember the word of the prophet:
　　Thou dost keep him in perfect peace,
　　whose mind is stayed on thee,
　　because he trusts in thee.　　　　　　　　*Isaiah 26.3*

I am trusting thee, Lord Jesus;
Never let me fall;
I am trusting thee for ever,
and for all.

O God,
I know that recovery cannot be quick.
I know that the body
takes its own time to heal.
But I know
    that everything possible
        is being done for me.
All the same
    I get impatient.
I want
    to be on my feet;
I want
    to get home again;
I want
    to get back to my work.
O God,
    teach me what I know already.
Teach me
    that the more impatient I am,
    the more I delay my recovery.
Help me to learn to wait
    cheerfully and hopefully and uncomplainingly,
        content to live one day
        and to take one step
            at a time.

Let me remember the Psalmist:
    Wait for the Lord;
    be strong, and let your heart take courage;
    yea, wait for the Lord!   *Psalm 27.14*

Trust in the Lord, for ever trust,
    and banish all your fears;
Strength in the Lord Jehovah dwells
    eternal as his years.

O God,
I'm all right
so long as I am lying here in bed,
or so long as I don't try to do anything;
   but I have just no strength.
I can't hurry;
   I can't even do anything quickly;
   I have always to take my time—
      and it is a long time.
It is so discouraging
   always to feel weak,
   and always to feel tired.
I want to get back to work,
   there is so much that I want to do,
   and so much that is waiting to be done.
O God,
give me the patience
that I know I must have.
Make me a little better every day,
and able to do a little more each day,
   until, bit by bit,
   I can shoulder the tasks of life again.

The prophet said:
   They who wait for the Lord shall renew their strength.
                                                 Isaiah 40.31

   O God, make this true for me.

Art thou weary, art thou languid,
   Art thou sore distressed?
'Come to me' saith One, 'and coming,
   Be at rest.'

42

O God,
When I think about myself,
  I am ashamed of myself.
Because I am so nervous and afraid,
  I am more demanding
    than I have any right to be.
Because I have become selfish,
  because all my life people have been too good to me,
    I think that no one matters but me.
Because I am far too self-willed,
  I don't co-operate as I ought
    with those who are doing their best for me.
Sometimes—often—I can be
  impatient, complaining, discontented,
  ungrateful, disobedient.
O God,
I can see all this,
  when I lie thinking about myself.
But somehow I do the things
  I don't want to do,
and I behave in a way that I know is wrong
  even when I am doing it.
Help me to conquer myself.
Give me
  patience, serenity, unselfishness,
  obedience, contentment, gratitude
    for all that is done for me.
Help me
  from now on not to be difficult,
  but to try to make things easier
    for those who are doing so much for me.

Let me take to myself the advice to Timothy:
  Aim at righteousness, godliness, faith, love, steadfastness,
  gentleness.   *I Timothy 6.11*

Hidden in the hollow
  Of his blessed hand,
Never foe can follow,
  Never traitor stand;

Not a surge of worry,
  Not a shade of care,
Not a blast of hurry,
  Touch the spirit there.

O God,
Even when I am lying here like this in bed,
  help me to count my blessings.
I can still talk,
  and use my hands quite a bit.
I can still send my mind and my imagination
  where my body can't go.
I can still remember,
  and I can still pray.
Help me
  not to grumble,
  not to complain,
  not to whine.
Keep me cheerful,
  and help me to make things as easy as I can
  for the people who have to look after me,
  and the people who come to see me.
And when things get so bad
  that I do want to break down and to break out,
help me to do it
  when there is no one there to see it but you,
  because I know you will understand.
Even on this bed
  give me the joy
    that nothing and no one can take from me.

Help me to remember and to believe what Jesus promised:
  So you have sorrow now, but I will see you again, and
  your hearts will rejoice, and no one will take your joy
  from you.   *John 16.22*

Nor death, nor life, nor earth, nor hell,
  nor time's destroying sway,
Shall e'er efface us from his heart,
  or make his love decay.

O God,
Sometimes I can't help wondering
why this should have happened to me.
You get a lot of time to think
   when you are lying in a hospital bed,
and you see a lot of things
   in a hospital.
And sometimes I can't help wondering
   why there is so much suffering and pain
     in the world.
I know that there just isn't any answer to these questions,
   at least just now.
So help me to accept
   what I can't understand.
And help me to be sure
   that this is not the only world,
and that there is some place
   where the broken things are mended,
   where the lost things are found,
   where all the questions are answered,
   where all the problems are solved,
   where we know, even as we are known.
So in this world help me
   to leave it all to you,
in the certainty that I will never be tried
   beyond what you will make me able to bear.

Give me the Psalmist's certainty:
   Even though I walk through the valley of the shadow of
     death,
   I will fear no evil; for thou art with me; thy rod and
   they staff, they comfort me.   *Psalm 23.4* AV

In heavenly love abiding,
   No change my heart shall **fear**;
And safe is such confiding,
   For nothing changes here:

The storm may roar without me,
　My heart may low be laid;
But God is round about me,
　And can I be dismayed?

✍ For courage ✍

Give me, O God,
  All the courage I need in this place.
Give me courage
  To bear discomfort without grumbling,
    and pain without complaint.
Give me courage
  To bear uncertainty with hope,
    and long delays with patience.
Give me courage
  To keep on trusting when I cannot understand,
And help me always to remember
  that, in this as in everything,
  it is the one who sticks it out gallantly to the end
  who will be saved.

Let me remember the word of Jesus:
  He who endures to the end will be saved.   *Matthew 24.13*

Sun of our life, thy quickening ray
Sheds on our path the glow of day;
Star of our hope, thy softened light
Cheers the long watches of the night.

O God,
I'm beginning to feel
that I'm losing the battle.
My strength just won't come back,
and this body of mine is tired.
I know
that they are doing their best for me.
I know
that those who love me
are thinking of me
and praying for me
all the time.
If it be possible,
help me to pass the breaking-point
and not to break,
but, sunshine or shadow,
I leave it to you.

Let me remember the confidence of the Psalmist:
Even though I walk through the valley of deep darkness,
I fear no evil, for thou art with me.   *Psalm 23.4*

Thine arm, O Christ, in days of old
Was strong to help and save;
It triumphed o'er disease and death,
O'er darkness and the grave.
Be thou our great deliverer still,
Thou Lord of life and death;
Restore and quicken, soothe and bless,
With thine almighty breath.

O God,
Sometimes I can't help feeling
  that I am one of these people Jesus meant
  when he talked about
  those who had little faith.
I am afraid of what might happen,
and I haven't the faith that can face the future
without a tremor.
Doubts get into my mind and heart,
and I sometimes wonder
if you do really care for me.
I suppose that, when illness like this comes,
far more people than I wonder
why this should have happened to them.
Sometimes I wonder if you can possibly hear my prayers.
There are so many people praying to you all at the one time.
And yet I know that
I wouldn't be alive at all, and
I couldn't have faced life at all
by myself.
And after all I wouldn't be talking to you now
unless I had some faith.
Give me the perfect and serene confidence
which can lean back and say:
Into your hands I commit my spirit,
for life and for death and for life to come.

Help me to remember the prayer that at least I can pray:
  I believe: help my unbelief!   *Mark 9.24*

Other refuge have I none;
  Hangs my helpless soul on thee;
Leave, ah! leave me not alone;
  Still support and comfort me.

50

O God,
Help me to say:
  Your will be done.
Help me
  to be quite sure
    that all things do work together for good.
Help me to remember and to discover
  that even pain and weakness
    can bring me nearer you,
  and that the dews of sorrow
    can be lustred by your love.
Help me to remember
  that it is your promise,
    that neither I nor anyone else
  will be tested above what we can bear.
Help me to remember
  that a father's hand will never cause
    his child a needless tear.
Help me
  to say, as my Blessed Lord said,
    Into your hands I commit my spirit.

Let me remember Jesus' last prayer:
  Father, into your hands I commit my spirit.   *Luke 23.46*

Not mine, not mine the choice,
  In things or great or small;
Be thou my guide and strength,
  My wisdom and my all.

O God,
It is very difficult to keep on hoping,
  when nothing seems to be happening.
And it is even more difficult
  when there seem to be more setbacks than progress.
Help me to have the hope
  that nothing can put out.
After all, even on the darkest night,
  no one ever doubts
    that the morning will come again;
and in the hardest winter
  no one ever doubts
    that spring is never far behind.
Help me to think
  of the skill you have given
    to those whose task it is to heal,
and of the essential toughness
  of this human body of mine.
Help me to remember
  that for you and with you
    nothing is impossible.
And help me to remember always
  that I have a hope
    that does not stop with this world,
      but goes on for ever.

Let me remember the Psalmist's confidence:
  Why are you cast down, O my soul,
  and why are you disquieted within me?
  Hope in God; for I shall again praise him,
  my help and my God.   *Psalm 43.5*

If thou but suffer God to guide thee,
  And hope in him through all thy ways,
He'll give thee strength, whate'er betide thee,
  And bear thee through the evil days;
Who trusts in God's unchanging love
Builds on the rock that nought can move.

O God,
I want to thank you
   for bringing me this far along the road to recovery.
It is good to be able
   to get my feet on the floor again;
It is good to be able
   to do at least some things for myself again.
It is best of all
   just to have the joy
   of feeling well again.
O God,
keep me grateful,
   grateful to all the people
   who helped me back to health;
grateful to you
   for the way in which
   you have brought me through it all.
O God,
still give me patience.
Help me
   not to be in too big a hurry to do too much.
Help me
   to keep on doing what I'm told to do.
Help me
   to be so obedient to those who know
   what is best for me, that very soon
   I shall be on the top of the world
   and on the top of my job again.

I can say what the Psalmist said:
   I waited patiently for the Lord;
   he inclined to me and heard my cry.   *Psalm 40.1*

He took me from a fearful pit,
   and from the miry clay,
And on a rock he set my feet,
   establishing my way.

O God,
It seems like yesterday
   that I went out to work for the first time;
and now I haven't much longer to go,
   and I'm well over the halfway line.
I can't shut my eyes to the fact
   that I'm getting older.
Physically, I get more easily tired,
   and any effort becomes more and more of an effort.
Mentally, I'm slower;
   I can't work for so long at a time;
     and concentration is more difficult.
First and foremost, help me to realise quite clearly
   what I can do and what I can't do,
   and to accept my necessary limitations.
And then help me to be thankful
   for all that the years have given me,
     and for all the experience that
     life has brought me.
Help me to use what is left to me of life
   wisely and well;
for time is short now,
   and I dare not waste any of it.

Let me remember what the prophet said:
   Your old men shall dream dreams,
   And your young men shall see visions.   *Joel 2.28*

Long as my life shall last,
   Teach me thy way!
Where'er my lot be cast,
   Teach me thy way!
Until the race is run,
Until the journey's done,
Until the crown is won,
   Teach me thy way!

O God,
I know now what it is like
to be growing old.
Everything is a bigger effort
than it used to be.
I get more easily tired,
and each job takes longer to do.
My memory is not so good;
My mind is not so quick;
My body is not so strong.
And yet I've got a lot to be thankful for.
I have learned
what is important
and what is not important.
I know now
that there are a great many things
not worth worrying about.
I have learned
to take the rough with the smooth
and not to get upset.
I have learned
who my real friends are,
and how much I owe to those who love me,
and to those whom I love.
Above all, when I look back
I can see your hand in everything,
and when I remember all that you have done for me
in the past
it's easy to trust you
for the days to come.

Isaiah heard God saying:
Even to your old age I am He,
and to grey hairs I will carry you,
I have made and I will bear;
I will carry and save.

Isaiah 46.4

Under the shadow of thy throne,
    Thy saints have dwelt secure;
Sufficient is thine arm alone,
    And our defence is sure.

O God,
I have come to the stage
  when I can no longer work,
    and when I can no longer even look after myself.
    I am not ill;
    I am just old.
  My body has no strength in it;
  my memory has grown forgetful;
  and sometimes my mind won't think.
Sometimes I feel very lonely,
  because there are so few
  of my friends and loved ones left.
And yet I have a lot to be thankful for.
  I have had a long day,
    and a good day's work.
  I am grateful that there are places like this,
    and I am grateful for the care of doctors and nurses
      who have devoted themselves
      to the care of those who are old;
    and I am grateful for the visits of people
      who have not forgotten me.
You have left me still here.
  Help me to accept life as it is;
and help me to live in the evening-time of life
  with cheerfulness and with serenity,
    and without complaint,
    until the day closes
      and you take me home to you.

Let the prayer of the Psalmist be my prayer:
  So even to old age and grey hairs,
  O God, do not forsake me.   *Psalm 71.18*

With mercy and with judgment
  My web of time he wove,
And aye the dews of sorrow
  Were lustred by his love;

I'll bless the hand that guided,
   I'll bless the heart that planned,
When throned where glory dwelleth
   In Immanuel's land.

O God,
I don't want anything startling or heroic;
I just want to be able to bear things.
They can do a lot for me,
but sometimes even their drugs don't work.
Help me to bear things
  without grumbling;
  without complaining;
  without whining;
  without self-pity,
    like a good soldier.
Help me
  to pass the breaking-point and not to break,
You know all about it, Lord Jesus.
You knew
  the mental agony of Gethsemane.
You knew
  the physical pain of the lash,
  of the crown of thorns, of the nails.
I know that you won't mind me saying
  that I'm glad you went through it all,
  because it means that you can understand
    exactly how I feel.
I know that in the end
  all things pass;
Till then, make me brave.
I wait for your promise of the time
  when there will be no more pain.

The Psalmist said:
  I kept my faith, even when I said, I am greatly afflicted.
  Help me too to keep my faith.   *Psalm 116.10*

No pain that we can share
But he has felt its smart,
All forms of human grief and care
Have pierced that tender heart.

O God,
I think that the trouble about lying here like this
    is that I am more worried about other people
    than I am about myself.
I can't help thinking what is going to happen
    to my wife and children,
    with so much less money coming in.
I can't help wondering what will happen
    if I come out of here
    not able for my old job.
I can't help wondering what will happen
    to those who depend on me
    if I don't come out at all.
It's all very well to talk
    about peace and not worrying,
But I wouldn't be human
    if I didn't feel like this—
    and I'm quite sure you understand.
But help me all the same to remember
    that, if I worry,
I am only making things worse,
    and spoiling my own chances.
So help me
    to take it one day at a time,
    and to leave the unknown future to you.

Let me remember the words of Jesus:
    Do not be anxious about tomorrow, for tomorrow will be
    anxious for itself. Let the day's own troubles be sufficient
    for the day.   *Matthew* 6.34

I know now what the future hath
    Of marvel or surprise,
Assured alone that life and death
    His mercy underlies.

O God,
It is hard to think of a world
  in which I cannot see the sun and the flowers,
  and the faces of those I love.
It is hard to think of a life
  in which I cannot read or watch things,
  or see lovely things any more.
But even in the dark there will be something left.
I can still have memory,
  and I can still see things again
  with my mind's eye.
I thank you for all that skill and kindness
  do for people like me.
I thank you for Braille, which keeps the world of books
  from being altogether closed to me.
I thank you that I will still be able
  to hear the voices that I know
  and to touch the things and the people I love.
Lord Jesus you are the Light of Life;
  Be with me in the dark.

Let me remember what Jesus said:
  I am the light of the world; he who follows me
  will not walk in darkness, but will have the light
    of life.   *John 8.12*

Light of the world! for ever, ever shining,
  There is no change in thee;
True Light of Life, all joy and health enshrining
  Thou canst not fade nor flee.

O God,
I cannot speak to you in words,
but I can still send my thoughts to you;
  and, although I can't say the words out loud,
  I know that you will hear.
Life can be very difficult
  when you can't speak.
Not to be able to tell people what I want;
Not to be able to ask or answer a question;
Not to be able to talk to friends and dear ones;
  To have the barrier of silence on my lips—
    It is very difficult.
Thank you, O God, for what is left—
  for writing;
  for the language of signs;
  for those who have learned to read my lips.
Help me to bear this that has happened to me,
and to accept it and not to feel frustrated.
Thank you
  for the people who are kind to me;
Thank you
  for making me sure
    that you can hear the words
    that I can't speak,
    and the things I can think
      but can not say.

Let me remember that words are unnecessary with God, for,
as the Psalmist said to God:
  Thou discernest my thoughts from afar.   *Psalm 139.2*

Prayer is the burden of a sigh,
  The falling of a tear,
The upward glancing of an eye
  When none but God is near.

O God,
The trouble about being deaf is that most people
find deaf people just a nuisance.
They sympathise with people
who are blind and lame;
but they just get irritated and annoyed
with people who are deaf.
And the result of this is
that deaf people are apt to avoid company,
and so get more and more lonely,
and more and more shut in.
Help me now that my hearing has begun to go.
Help me
    to face the situation
    and to realise that there is no good
        trying to hide it,
    for that will only make it worse and worse.
Help me
    to be grateful for all that can be done
    for deaf people like me.
If I have got to wear a hearing-aid,
    Help me to do it quite naturally,
    and not be shy or embarrassed about it.
Give me the perseverance
    not to let this trouble get me down,
    and not to let it cut me off from others.
And help me to remember
    that, whatever happens,
    there is nothing can stop me hearing your voice.

Even if I cannot hear the voices of men, let me remember
Samuel and say:
    Speak, for thy servant hears.   *I Samuel 3.10*

Hear him ye deaf; his praise, ye dumb,
    Your loosened tongues employ;
Ye blind, behold your Saviour come;
    And leap, ye lame, for joy!

63

O God,
Sometimes I can't help thinking
    about the things I miss,
because I am tied to this house,
    and can't move around now.
I miss the open air and the open road,
    and the feel of the sun and the wind and the rain.
I miss going to work and going to the shops.
I miss playing and watching games.
I miss the church on Sunday.
Still, I know that I have a lot of things left.
My body may be tied to the one place,
    but I can still send my mind and my thoughts
        and my imagination
        adventuring anywhere.
I've got books to read,
    radio to listen to, television to watch,
I've got good friends
    who never forget to come to see me.
Help me to remember that,
    even if I can't be anything else,
I can at least be cheerful.
Help me not to be too sorry for myself,
    and always to keep smiling.

Let me remember the Psalmist:
    The Lord lifts up those who are bowed down. *Psalm 146.8*

Rest of the weary, joy of the sad;
Hope of the dreary, light of the glad;
Home of the stranger, strength to the end;
Refuge from danger, Saviour and friend.

O God,
I never thought when I went out that morning
that I would finish up here in this hospital.
Now I really know
    that life is an uncertain business,
and that you never know
    what is going to happen.
I don't really know whether the whole thing was my fault,
    or whether someone else was to blame.
Don't let me start wondering about that.
Just let me accept this,
    and do everything I can
    to help my own progress.
Help those who love me
    to get over the shock
    that this must have been to them.
Help them not to worry,
    but to be sure
    that I'm in good hands here.
And when I get out of here
    help me to remember to be a lot more careful,
    so that I won't get involved in an accident,
    and so that I won't be the cause of an accident
    to anyone else.
I am very grateful that I am still alive,
    and that things are no worse than they are.
Help me to be a good patient
    so that I will soon be on my feet again.

The Sage was right when he said:
    You do not know what a day may bring forth.

Proverbs 27.1

But in spite of that, help me to say:
Peace, perfect peace, our future all unknown?
Jesus we know, and he is on the throne.

O God,
The trouble about life just now
  is that I seem to have all the things
  which don't matter,
    and I seem to have lost all the things
    which do matter.
I have life;
  I have money enough to live on;
    I have a job to do;
but I am alone,
  and sometimes I feel that nothing
    can make up for that.
O God,
compel me to see the meaning of my faith.
  Make me realise that
    I have a hope as well as a memory;
  that the unseen cloud of witnesses is around me;
    that Jesus meant it when he said
    that he would always be with me.
And make me realise that
  so long as you leave me here
there is something that I am meant to do;
  and in doing it, help me to find
    the comfort and the courage
    that I need to go on.

Let me remember Paul's confidence:
  But we would not leave you ignorant, brethren, concerning
  those who are asleep, that you may not grieve as others do
  who have no hope. For since we believe that Jesus died and
  rose again, even so, through Jesus, God will bring with him
  those who have fallen asleep.   *I Thessalonians 4.13,14*

'Midst pastures green he'll lead his flock,
  Where living streams appear,
And God the Lord from every eye
  Shall wipe off every tear.

O God,
Help me to be grateful
  for the things which come so regularly
  that we can forget that they are gifts.
Help me to be grateful
  for the things which so often we do not value
    until we lose them.
Above all, make me grateful to you for my health,
  for strength of body and for health of mind,
  for accuracy of hand and eye,
    and mind and brain,
      to do my work.
Give me sympathy for those who are ill;
and help me never to be impatient and annoyed
  and irritated
    with those who are not so strong as I am.
Help me to give my strength to the weak,
and grant that my own good health
  may never make me forget,
    those who are less fortunate than I am.

Job said:
  I was eyes to the blind,
  and feet to the lame,
  I was a father to the poor.   *Job 29.15,16*
May that be my aim too.

My health and friends and parents dear
  To me by God are given;
I have not any blessing here
  But what is sent from heaven.

O God,
I needn't tell you how difficult . . . is.
He is irritable and impatient and demanding;
    whatever I do is wrong.
      He wouldn't be happy
      unless he had something to complain about.
    He will never even admit
      that he is making progress
      and feeling better.
O God,
give me patience,
    never to let myself be angered and upset;
give me sympathy,
    always to try to understand;
give me wisdom of mind,
    to help him through his difficult time.
Keep me from becoming annoyed,
    no matter what the provocation;
and help me always to keep on caring,
    even when there seems to be no response.
Hasten his/her cure
    in body and in mind,
so that the day will soon come
when the difficult time will be forgotten.
And, Lord Jesus, help me always to remember,
    that, whatever I have to bear,
it is nothing to the ingratitude and the thanklessness
    that you had to bear.

Let me think of what Peter said to those who had to work for
others :
    Servants, be submissive to your masters with all respect, not
    only to the kind and gentle but also to the overbearing . . .
    For what credit is it, if when you do wrong and are beaten
    for it you take it patiently? But if when you do right and
    suffer for it you take it patiently, you have God's approval
                                                    I Peter 2.18-20

Though long the weary road we tread,
   And sorrow crown each lingering year,
No path we shun, no darkness dread,
   Our hearts still whispering, ' Thou art near.'

O God,
I know that when I get back home
life is never going to be quite the same again.
I know
   that I will always have to take care;
   and that I will have to go much slower;
   and that I will not be able to make the efforts
     that I used to make.
Help me to be glad that I am as I am,
   and that I have got what I have.
I am still alive, and I can still work;
I can still move about;
I can still meet my friends,
   and see the beauty of the world.
I can see now
   that I was living at far too fast a pace,
   and at far too great a pressure.
So help me from now on
   to accept life as it is,
   and to make the best of it.
And help me to be sure that,
   if I go about it in the right way,
   life is not finished,
   but that the best is yet to be.

Let me remember what Paul said:
   I have learned, in whatever state I am, to be content.
Philippians 4.11

I am content with what I have,
   Little be it or much;
And, Lord, contentment still I crave,
   Because thou savest such.

O God,
Keep me from praying to you,
as if there was no one in this ward except me.
Help me to remember
  that I am only one person and one voice
  in this ward and in this hospital,
    and in a world in which
      there are so many people in trouble.
Bless everyone in this ward,
  Anyone who is lonely or frightened,
    anyone who is shy and nervous;
  anyone who is suffering a lot of pain;
    anyone who is making slow progress
      and who is discouraged;
  anyone who has had a setback today
    and who is disappointed;
  anyone who is worried and anxious;
    anyone for whom there is no recovery.
And help me to help others,
  and so to forget my own troubles,
  by sharing the troubles of others.

Let me remember Paul's advice:
  Bear one another's burdens, and so fulfil the law of Christ.
                                        Galatians 6.2

In sickness, sorrow, want or care,
Whate'er it be, 'tis ours to share;
May we, where help is needed, there
  Give help as unto thee.

O God,
The months of waiting are ended,
  and my time is almost here.
Take away all tension and fear,
  and make me relaxed and unafraid.
Strengthen me for my ordeal,
  and give me joy in remembering
  that through me you are sending
    another life into this world.

I remember that Jesus said:
  When a woman is in travail she has sorrow, because her
  hour has come; but when she is delivered of the child,
  she no longer remembers the anguish, for joy that a child
  is born into the world.   *John 16.21*

O Father, Thou who has created all
  In wisest love, we pray,
Look on this babe, who at Thy gracious call
  Is entering on life's way;
Bend o'er him in Thy tenderness,
Thine image on his soul impress;
  O Father, hear.

O God,
Thank you
  for bringing me and my baby
    safely through everything.
Bless my baby.
  Keep him/her safe
    in all the dangers of childhood.
  Bring him/her in safety to manhood/womanhood;
    and grant that some day
      he/she may do a good day's work in the world;
  and help me always to help him/her to see
    that Jesus is his/her friend.
Bless me.
  You have given me this great privilege;
  help me now to be true to my great responsibility,
    and never to fail in the trust you have given to me.
Help me, when I get home again,
  to make my home a place
  where Jesus is an unseen
    but an always remembered guest.

I remember today how Jesus said:
  Whoever receives one such child in my name receives me.
                               Matthew 18.5

Grant us, then, pure hearts and patient,
  That, in all we do or say,
Little souls our deeds may copy,
  And be never led astray;
Little feet our steps may follow
  In a safe and narrow way.

Lord Jesus
　　It is my great comfort to know
　　　　that, where I have been,
　　　　you have been before.
You had a day's work to do
　　just as I have a day's work to do.
You were tempted
　　just as I am tempted.
You were distressed in mind in Gethsemane
　　just as I am distressed in mind.
You had to suffer pain
　　just as I have to suffer pain
　　and your pain was far worse than mine.
You are the Resurrection and the Life,
　　because you died and rose again,
　　and you are alive always and for ever,
　　　　and once and for all you conquered death.
So I am quite sure that, whatever happens to me,
　　you have been there;
　　you are there;
　　you will be there,
　　　　to the end of time and beyond.

Jesus said to Martha:
　　I am the Resurrection and the Life; he who believes in
　　me, though he die, yet shall he live, and whoever lives
　　and believes in me shall never die.　　　　*John 11.25,26*

Thou art the Way, the Truth, the Life:
　Grant us that way to know
That truth to keep, that life to win,
　　Whose joys eternal flow.

*A thanksgiving for Jesus the Good Physician and for all
who follow in His steps*

O God,
I thank you for Jesus, the Good Physician.
  I thank you that he restored
    health to men's bodies
    and sanity to their minds.
  I thank you that he cared
    for all who were in pain of body
    and in distress of mind.
  I thank you for all doctors
    who follow in his steps;
    for all who have studied and toiled and experimented
      to find a cure for disease;
    for all who have risked their life and their health
      that others might be healed;
    for all who have skill to heal the body;
    for all who have patience to minister to minds
      which have lost their balance;
    for those whose quiet, calm strength
      stills men's fears,
      when they are worried and in pain.
    Give to all engaged in the work of healing
      the joy of knowing that they do the work
        of Jesus, the Good Physician.

Jesus said:
  Those who are well have no need of a physician but those
  who are sick . . . I came not to call the righteous but
  sinners.   *Matthew 9.12,13*

Where'er they heal the maimed and blind,
  Let love of Christ attend,
Proclaim the Good Physician's mind,
  And prove the Saviour Friend.
For Christ the Lord can now employ
  As agents of his will,
Restoring health and strength and joy,
  The doctor's love and skill.

75

O God,
I have learned a lot
  since I came to this bed.
I have learned the uncertainty of life,
  that we cannot tell what a day will bring;
I have learned the weakness of life,
  that I am a frail creature at the best.
I have learned that I am not indispensable,
  that life gets on well enough without me,
  which is both humiliating and comforting.
I have learned a lot about you.
  I have learned to see your hand
    when things go badly
  just as much as when they go well;
  that the shadows are yours just as much
    as the sunshine.
  I have learned that
    the more I need you, the more you are there.
I know now that
  you do work all things together for good,
  and that you do love me with an everlasting love.

I too can say:
  Hitherto the Lord has helped me.   *I Samuel 7.12*

Every joy or trial
  Falleth from above,
Traced upon our dial
  By the Sun of Love.
We may trust him fully
  All for us to do;
They who trust him wholly
  Find him wholly true.

O God,
I thank you that there are such places as
  hospitals and infirmaries and nursing-homes.
I thank you for those who have the skill
  to find out what is wrong
  and to put it right again.
I thank you for those
  who throughout the day and night
  attend to those in discomfort, distress and pain.
I thank you that there are places
  where the ill and the weak and the old
  are not looked on as a nuisance,
  but where they find
  loving care and attention.
I thank you
  not only for doctors and surgeons and nurses,
  but for all the people who do the many jobs
  which have to be done, if the work of the hospital is to go
  on—
  technicians, dispensers, dieticians,
  social service workers, nurses' aides, orderlies,
  secretaries, typists, clerks,
  porters, ambulance drivers,
  cooks and kitchen maids.
Help me to remember
  all those who are helping you
  to make me well again,
  and to give thanks for them.

Help all who work in hospitals to remember what Jesus said:
  Truly, I say to you, as you did it to one of the least of these
  my brethren, you did it to me.   *Matthew 25.40*

To comfort and to bless,
To find a balm for woe,
To tend the lone and fatherless,
  Is angels' work below.

77

O God,
I ask you to bless
   all those who care for me in this hospital.
Bless the surgeons and the physicians.
I thank you
   for the knowledge and for the skill
   which you have given to them.
Bless the nurses.
I thank you
   for their cheerfulness and their patience and their
   watchfulness all through the day and night.
Bless those who cook the meals
   and who clean the wards,
   and carry out the endless administrative duties
   that a place like this needs.
Give to all who care for the sick,
   not only here but in all hospitals and infirmaries
   and nursing-homes
   joy and satisfaction in their work.
And when they get tired of their work,
And a bit fed up with people like me,
   help them to remember how great a thing it is
     to ease the pains
     and heal the bodies of suffering men and women.
And help them never to forget
Jesus who healed all those who had need of healing.

Let me remember what the Gospel tells me about Jesus:
   That evening they brought to him many who were pos-
   sessed with demons; and he cast out the spirits with a
   word, and healed all who were sick. This was to fulfil
   what was spoken by the prophet Isaiah: He took out
   infirmities and bore our diseases.   *Matthew 8.16,17*

From thee all skill and science flow,
   All pity, care, and love.
All calm and courage, faith and hope;
   O pour them from above.

For hospital visitors and chaplains

O God,
I ask you to bless
all hospital chaplains,
and all who come to visit people
    in hospitals and in infirmaries and in nursing-homes.
Give them sympathy
    so that they may really and truly enter
        into the anxieties and the fears and the pains
            of those they visit.
Give them cheerfulness,
    so that their visit
        may be like a ray of sunshine.
Give them insight
    so that they may know
        when to stay
        and when to go.
    Help them never to visit just as a duty,
    but to come because they really care
    and really want to help.
And, when they come,
    help them to bring with them,
    something of that Master and Lord
        to whom men and women and children upon earth
            came for help and healing.

May those who visit those in trouble remember the prophet's
word:
    The Spirit of the Lord God is upon me,
    because the Lord has anointed me
    to bring good tidings to the afflicted.   *Isaiah 61.1*

From Thee all skill and science flow,
    All pity, care, and love,
All calm and courage, faith and hope;
    O pour them from above.

O God,
This is the day
    when operations are carried out.
Help those who have to go to the operating room today
    not to be too nervous or anxious or frightened.
Help them to trust
    in the kindness and the efficiency of the nurses,
    the wisdom of the anaesthetist,
    the skill and the knowledge of the doctors and the surgeons.
And help them to remember
    that you are just as near them in an operating room
        as you are in any church.
Help the rest of us who have already been through things
    to help those who have to go through them.
Help them to know that it is worth anything to be well again,
    and to remember that nothing
        in life or in death
        can separate them from you.
Help those at home
    not to worry too much.
We cannot help being anxious
    when our loved ones are ill.
But help us in confidence and in calmness
    to leave everything
    to the healing skill of men,
    and to your love.

Let me say what the Psalmist said:
    When I am afraid,
    I put my trust in thee.   *Psalm 56.3*

The Lord's my light and saving health,
    who shall make me dismay'd?
My life's strength is the Lord, of whom
    then shall I be afraid?

ᘐ A prayer for a hospital receiving day ᘐ

O God,
This is the day when the new patients
  come into this ward.
I know how they are feeling,
  uncertain, strange, apprehensive,
  nervous, worried, downright afraid.
Help me to do everything I can
  to help them.
Help me
  to try to welcome
    those who are shy;
  to try to calm
    those who are nervous;
  to try to help
    those who are afraid not to worry.
In this ward we are a lot of bits and pieces of
  humanity flung together,
  because we all happen to have something wrong
    with us.
While we are here
  make us one family,
  so that no one who comes in
  will be left feeling a stranger.

The Psalmist said:
  The Lord preserveth the strangers.   *Psalm 146.9* AV

In sickness, sorrow, want, or care,
Whate'er it be, 'tis ours to share;
May we where help is needed, there
  Give help as unto Thee.

O God,
This is the day
   when a lot of people in this ward
   are going to be allowed to go back home.
     And I can't help envying them.
It's not that I grudge it to them,
and it's not that I don't appreciate
   all that is done for me here,
   but home is home, and there's no place like it.
All the same, help me to be glad
   because they are glad.
There is nothing like the joy
   of meeting after separation,
and wives and husbands, parents and children,
   will be meeting again tonight.
Keep them from too much excitement,
   and from trying to do too much at first,
   and from all discouragements and setbacks.
Help me to be so good a patient,
   that I too will soon get home,
   and when the new patients come in,
help me like a veteran soldier
   to do my best to help
     those who are beginning the battle
     to be well.

Let me learn, as Paul wanted his friends to learn,
   to rejoice with those who rejoice,
   and to weep with those who weep.   *Romans 12.15*

Still the weary, sick, and dying
   Need a brother's, sister's care;
On Thy higher help relying
   May we now their burden share.

O God,
Help me all through today.
Help me
  to be grateful for any progress,
    however little.
Help me
  not to be discouraged by any setbacks,
    however disappointing.
Help me
  to be easy to help,
  so that the doctors and nurses
    may find me a good patient.
Help me
  to help others
    who are also going through it,
      by being cheerful and sympathetic.
Make me a good listener,
  more ready to listen to other people's troubles
  than to talk about my own.
So help me to live through today in such a way
  that at evening
  I will have nothing to regret.

Let me share the prophet's faith and gratitude:
  The steadfast love of the Lord never ceases,
    his mercies never come to an end;
  they are new every morning;
    great is thy faithfulness.   *Lamentations 3.22,23*

We cannot tell what gladness
  May be our lot today,
What sorrow or temptation
  May meet us on our way;
But this we know most surely,
  That, through all good or ill,
God's grace can always help us
  To do His Holy will.

O God,
Thank you
  for all that has been done for me today.
Thank you
  for the people who looked after my body,
    and my meals.
Thank you
  for the people who thought out
    the treatment that I need,
  and for the people
    who gave it to me.
Thank you for the people
whose minds took thought for me,
  and whose hands cared for me.
Forgive me, if at any time today
  I have been cross and impatient,
  unreasonable or unco-operative.
Forgive me, if I did anything
  to make the work of others harder,
  and my own recovery slower.
Thank you
  for the friendships we have made in this ward,
Specially bless and help . . . and . . . and . . .
Help me now to sleep well,
and to waken refreshed tomorrow.

Let me think of the Psalmist's faith:
  He will give his angels charge of you
  to guard you in all your ways.   *Psalm 91.11*

Now God be with us, for the night is closing;
The light and darkness are of His disposing,
And 'neath His shadow here to rest we yield us,
  For He will shield us.

*Prayers for Morning and Evening
for Fourteen Days in Hospital*

We have now given prayers for most of the special occasions of illness, but besides prayer for the special occasions, we need prayer for morning and evening each day, and so now we give prayers for morning and evening for fourteen days in hospital.

∽∾

FIRST DAY

Morning

O God,
Help me to live today well,
Help me
    to bear pain, if need be, uncomplainingly,
      and discomfort cheerfully.
Help me
    to cause as little trouble,
      and to give as much help as possible.
And help me today
    to take one step forward
    on the road back to health.
    This I ask for Jesus' sake.   A M E N

Evening

O God,
Thank you for everything that has been done for me
by anyone in this hospital today,
    and thank you for those
    who have come to visit me.
Thank you
    for everything that has helped me
      to become more healthy in body,
        and more cheerful and contented in mind.
Help me now, even in this strange place,
    to sleep well,
      and bless all the people
        whom I am thinking of now.
        This I ask for your love's sake.   A M E N

SECOND DAY

Morning

Give me today, O God,
  the grace of friendliness,
    that I may gladly share the troubles and the joys
    of those who are in this place with me.
Give me grace to speak the right word,
  when I speak,
    and to know when to be silent and to listen
    to someone else who wants to talk.
Help us all in this place
  to come to know each other better today,
  and so in new friendship
    to find new strength.
    This I ask for Jesus' sake.   **AMEN**

Evening

Forgive me, O God,
  if today I have been depressed myself,
    and if I have depressed anyone else.
Forgive me,
  if there has been complaint on my lips,
    and discontent in my mind.
Forgive me,
  if I have not taken my share of suffering
    like a good soldier of Jesus Christ.
Give me tonight restful sleep,
  and grant that tomorrow I may awake
    stronger in body
    and more serene in mind.
    This I ask for Jesus' sake.   **AMEN**

THIRD DAY

Morning

O God,
Lying in bed gives me a chance to do things
that I did not have much chance to do before.
When I am lying here not able to do things,
  help me to use this time
    to take a good look at myself,
    so that I will know myself better than I did.
Help me to use it
  to take a good look at the life that I was living,
  so that when I get back to it
    I may make a better job of
    getting things in their right proportions.
Help me to use this time
  to read your Book.
I have always been too busy to read it up to now,
  Help me to find out
    what the Bible really says.
So grant that at the end of this time
I may have a fitter body and a more honest mind,
and a heart stayed more firmly on you.
This I ask for Jesus' sake.   AMEN

Evening

O God,
Before I sleep I remember before you
  all the people I love,
and now in the silence
  I say their names to you.
I remember before you
all the people who are
  sad and lonely,
  old and forgotten,
  poor and hungry and cold,
  in pain of body and in distress of mind.
Bless all who specially need your blessing,
  and bless me too, and make this
    a good night for me.
This I ask for your love's sake.   AMEN

FOURTH DAY

Morning

O God,
I used to wake up eager for each day,
and looking forward to every minute of it.
    Then I got tireder and tireder,
    and the days became things
    to be wearily got through somehow or other.
That is what brought me in here to hospital.
    Help me to be a good patient,
    so that when I leave hospital
    each day will be a thrill again
    and not a weariness.
    This I ask for your love's sake.   AMEN

Evening

O God,
Do for me all that I need done for me tonight.
    Rest my body and ease my pain;
    Calm my mind and stop my thoughts
    going round and round in anxious circles.
Take from me the fears and the uncertainties
    and the nervousness;
and give me faith
    to trust the doctors
    and to trust you.
    This I ask for your love's sake.   AMEN

FIFTH DAY
Morning

O God,
Help me to live one day at a time,
   not to be thinking of what might have been
     and not to be worrying about what may be.
Help me to accept the fact
   that I cannot undo the past,
   and I cannot foresee the future.
But even as I think of this,
and even as I face today,
help me always to remember
   that I will never be tried beyond what I can bear;
   that a father's hand will never cause
     his child a needless tear;
   that I cannot ever drift
     beyond your love and care.
So help me to live today
in courage, in cheerfulness and in peace.
This I ask for Jesus' sake.

AMEN

Evening

O God,
I thank you
   for everyone who spoke to me today,
     and for everyone who even smiled at me in the passing.
I thank you
   for everyone who made me feel
     that they were really interested in me,
     and that they were really wishing me well.
I thank you for the people
   who, I know, are thinking of me now,
   and praying for me now.
Bless the people at home
   who are missing me and worrying about me,
and grant that it may not be long
   until they and I are together again.
This I ask for Jesus' sake.

AMEN

SIXTH DAY

Morning

O God,
You have given me today;
give me also strength and grace
   to live it well.
Keep me today
   both from selfishness and from self-pity.
Help me always to remember
   that I am not the only one
      who needs attention;
   and that I am not the only one
      who is in trouble.
Help me always to be thankful for what is done for me,
   and never to be critical of it;
and make me full of gratitude
   and not of complaints.
All through the day help me to see
   the bright and not the dark side of things,
so that for me a happy heart
   may help to make a healthy body.
   This I ask for Jesus' sake.   AMEN

Evening

O God,
Bless all the people in this hospital tonight;
   those who are on the mend;
   those for whom life is drawing to its close;
   those who will sleep well;
   those who will lie awake, tense and nervous;
   nurses who will be on duty all night;
   doctors who will be called out when things go wrong.
And bless me.
   Help me to sleep well.
   Help me not to worry about myself,
      and not to worry about those I love,
But to leave them and myself
   in your hands.
   This I ask for your love's sake.   AMEN

SUNDAY

Morning

O God,
It is strange not being with the family today,
  and it's strange not going to church.
I miss the church,
  and I am grateful for the radio,
    and for the sermons on it.
I miss the family in the house today;
I miss the Sunday dinner with them all there;
I miss the family visits.
One thing is certain—
I'm going to value these things a lot more
  when I get out of here.
Even here, I can read my Bible
  and I can pray.
And you are here with me in this place
  just as much as you are in church.
So help me to feel even here
  that this is your day—the Lord's Day.
  This I ask for Jesus' sake.   AMEN

Evening

O God, thank you for today.
Thank you
  for the people who came to visit me,
  and for all the news they brought me.
Thank you
  for the sermons and the prayers and the hymns
  I have heard today on the radio.
Thank you
  for everyone who has thought of me today,
  and for everyone
    who has done anything for me today,
  and thank you for yourself
    and for your presence.
Give me now peace of body
  and peace of mind
    so that I may sleep well tonight.
    I ask it all for Jesus' sake.   AMEN

EIGHTH DAY

Morning

O God,
Thank you for the things
   which tell me that I am not forgotten.
Thank you
   for the letters and the get-well cards
   and the flowers and the gifts
   that people have sent to me,
   and brought to me.
I did not realise that these things
   could make such a difference.
When I get well again,
   grant that I may always remember
   my friends in hospital,
   and grant that I may always find some way
   of letting them know that I remember them.
Help me all through today
   to be cheerful and contented and brave,
and all through it make me sure
   of your presence and of your love.
   This I ask for Jesus' sake.   AMEN

Evening

O God,
I know that sleep is the best of all medicines,
   both for the body and the mind.
   Help me to sleep well tonight.
Take away all my fears and worries,
   all my tensions and my feeling of strangeness.
Give me
   a body that is relaxed,
   a mind that is at peace,
   a heart that is at rest.
Help me now to accept your invitation,
   and to cast all my burdens upon you,
and then help me to feel the everlasting arms
   underneath me and around me,
   always holding me close and safe:
   through Jesus Christ my Lord.   AMEN

NINTH DAY

Morning

O God, as I lie here,
I ask you to bless all the people
who are going out to work this morning,
   in the factories and the shipyards and the mines;
   in the offices and the shops and the class-rooms;
all the children going to school,
   and all the mothers starting the day's housework;
all the doctors and the surgeons and the nurses
 in their work
     of healing and easing pain.
And bless me,
   and help me today to become better and stronger,
   so that very soon I too will be back
     to the day's work.
     This I ask for Jesus' sake.   AMEN

Evening

O God,
Thank you,
   for all the people who looked after me today.
Thank you
   for all the people who came to visit me today.
Thank you
   for the newspapers and the books and the magazines
     I have read.
Thank you
   for all the care and the attention I have received,
     and for everyone who has helped me through today.
Now help me to sleep well
and to waken stronger.
This I ask for Jesus' sake.   AMEN

TENTH DAY

Morning

O God, take from me today
  all fear for myself,
    and all worry about others.
Give me patience,
  not to be in too big a hurry,
and give me cheerfulness,
  never to get depressed.
Help me to be
  relaxed in body,
  and at peace in mind.
I know that here
I am being treated with the best of knowledge and of skill.
  Help me myself to be such in mind and heart
    that I will get the best out of it.
    This I ask for your love's sake.   AMEN

Evening

O God,
When we are ill,
  the night hours are the long hours.
It is at night
  that fears are most frightening
  and worries most worrying.
Help me to sleep tonight,
  and, if I don't sleep,
  help me at least to relax and to rest.
Make me tonight
  sure of your presence
  and sure of your love.
  This I ask for Jesus' sake.   AMEN

ELEVENTH DAY

Morning

O God,
Help me this morning to think,
not of my own troubles,
    but of the troubles of others.
Bless those for whom today is going to be a difficult day;
    those who will have pain to bear;
    those to whom sorrow will come;
    those who will be involved in worry and anxiety;
    those who will have some
        specially difficult decision to take,
        or some specially difficult task to do.
I understand how they feel much better
    now that I have been through it myself.
Bless me, and help me, to live
    not even a day at a time,
        but to take each moment as it comes.
This I ask for your love's sake.   AMEN

Evening

O God, help me to go to sleep thinking of your promises.
The eternal God is your dwelling place;
    and underneath are the everlasting arms.
Help me to feel tonight
    the clasp of the love that will never let me go.
When you pass through the waters I will be with you.
Help me to feel you closest
    when life is sorest.
I will never fail you nor forsake you.
Help me to be very sure that, whatever happens,
    I do not have to face it alone.
Even the darkness is not dark to thee.
Help me to know that the darkest night
    is light, if you are there.
Help me tonight to believe in these promises and to rest
in them: through Jesus Christ my Lord.   AMEN
*(The texts are from Deuteronomy 33.27; Isaiah 43.2; Hebrews
13.5; Psalm 139.12)*

TWELFTH DAY

Morning

O God,
It won't be long now
   till I get home.
Thank you for bringing me this far
   along the way to health again.
Keep me patient and obedient
   right to the end of my stay here,
      so that there will be no last minute setbacks,
         and no disappointments,
   and don't let anything go wrong now.
   This I ask for your love's sake.   **AMEN**

Evening

O God,
Thank you for today.
Thank you
   for the people I have got to know,
      and the friendships I have made,
         since I came into this ward.
Thank you
   for the cheerful people,
      who keep us smiling;
   and for the helpful people
      who always find something to do for others.
Help me to take my share
   in making us all into one family in this ward.
   This I ask for Jesus' sake.   **AMEN**

THIRTEENTH DAY

Morning

O God,
I'm counting the days now,
  until it is time for me to go home.
Keep me from being impatient,
  and in too big a hurry.
Give me the common sense
  to give those who know best
  time to finish the job well and truly.
Help me to remember
  that a day or two extra now
  can save a long time later on.
Help me over the last lap
  now that the goal is in sight.
  This I ask for your love's sake.   AMEN

Evening

O God,
It is wonderful to think
  that very soon now
  I'll be sleeping in my own bed again,
  and wakening up in my own room again
    with all my own people round about me.
You have brought me safely through all this.
  My body is healed;
  my mind is at rest.
Give me one gift more—
  the gift of the grateful heart.
Tonight I go to sleep
  grateful for the past,
  and looking forward to the future—
    and I owe it all to you,
      and to those whose skill has healed me,
      and whose care has looked after me.
And so tonight with all my heart I thank you.
Hear this my prayer, through Jesus Christ my Lord.   AMEN

SUNDAY

Morning

O God,
Here in this hospital
  one day seems very like another.
But help me to remember
  that this is your day.
I cannot worship with your people in church today,
  so help me to worship here.
Help me,
  to think about you;
  to read your Book;
  to listen to a service on the radio;
  to pray this prayer to you.
Bless the people who go to church this morning.
  Give ministers a message to preach,
  and help the people in the congregation
    really to worship you,
      and help me to feel close to you
        on this your day.
  This I ask for Jesus' sake.   AMEN

Evening

O God,
Thank you
  for keeping me safe
    for another day.
Thank you
  for all that has been done for me today
    in this place.
Thank you
  for anything that has shown me
    that my friends still remember me,
    and that those who love me still care.
I know that the darkness and the light
  are both alike to you.
Help me in the dark hours to sleep in peace and in trust,
  and to waken tomorrow
  fitter to take up life again.
  This I ask for Jesus' sake.   AMEN

Prayers for Festivals
and Special Days

O God,
Thank you
  for allowing me to begin another year of life today.
Being ill has given me time to think.
I realise now
  how much time I have been wasting.
I realise now
  how ungrateful I have been,
    and how much I have been taking for granted.
I realise now
  how difficult I have been to live with.
I realise now
  that I needed something
    to bring me to my senses.
Today I make it my resolution
  to try to deserve better
    the gifts I receive.
Help me to keep it,
  both here,
    and when I get back to home and back to work.
This I ask for your love's sake. AMEN

O God,
I am glad that this is Easter Day.
I remember the hymn;
   Jesus Christ is risen today.
Help me to realise all that this means.
Help me to know that I am never alone.
In pain,
   he is here to help me to bear it.
In fear,
   he is here to help me to face it.
In loneliness,
   he is here to be my faithful friend;
In life,
   nothing can separate me from him.
If death comes,
   in him the conqueror of death is with me.
O God, give me this Easter faith today: through Jesus
Christ my Lord. AMEN

Lord Jesus,
I remember today
  how on the first Whitsunday
    your Spirit came in power to your disciples.
I remember
  how your Spirit gave the disciples
    courage and wisdom and power.
Give me your Spirit today,
  so that I too may be given
the courage
  to face anything that may happen to me
    and not to be afraid;
the wisdom
  to trust those who know best,
    and not to complain;
the power
  to conquer my own weakness,
    and with your help to win my way back to health.
Hear this my prayer for your love's sake. AMEN

O God,
At home tonight they are getting everything
   ready for Christmas Day.
They are hanging up the children's stockings,
   and laying out the presents,
      and getting ready for the Christmas dinner tomorrow.
      And this year I'm out of it all,
        and I'm wondering
      if they are missing me
        as much as I am missing them.
O God,
Help me not to get upset or depressed about this,
   because if I do I will only spoil things
      for myself and for everyone else.
Help me to look cheerful,
   even if I am not feeling cheerful.
Help me to remember
   that there are a lot of other people in this ward
   feeling just the same as I do,
and help us all to enjoy
Christmas Day together tomorrow:
   through Jesus Christ my Lord. AMEN

✎ *For Christmas Day* ✎

O God,
It is very strange to be away from home
  on Christmas Day,
and of course I can't help missing
all the things that happen in a home
  on Christmas Day.
But all the same I have a lot to be thankful for,
  and I know it.
Thank you
  for everything that has shown me
  that my friends and my family have not forgotten me.
Thank you
  for all the Christmas cards and presents
  that have come to me here.
Thank you
  for everything that the nurses and the doctors
    and the staff of this hospital have done
      to make this a real Christmas Day.
O God,
Help me to remember that Christmas Day
  is more than a day of presents and parties.
Help me to remember that this is the anniversary
  of the day when Jesus came into this world,
  to tell us of your love,
  and never to leave us any more.
All this I ask for your love's sake. AMEN

O God,
At the beginning of the year I never thought
   that at the end of it I would be here in this place.
It is just as well that we cannot see in advance
   what is going to happen to us.
Thank you,
   for everything that has happened this year.
Thank you,
   for the things
      which will always be happy memories.
Thank you,
   for the things
      which showed me my own weakness,
         and which kept me humble.
Thank you,
   for the things
      which compelled me to remember you,
         and to realise how much I need you.
Thank you,
   for the loyalty of friends
      and the faithfulness of loved ones.
Thank you
   even for this illness,
      which has shown me how kind people can be;
      which has made me appreciate
         the skill of doctors and the devotion of nurses;
      and which has made me realise
         what a gift good health is.
Hear this my prayer, for your love's sake. AMEN

Prayers for Those who are
Engaged in Healing

Paul Tournier in his book, A Doctor's Casebook in the Light of the Bible, *passes on to us the following sayings about those who are engaged in healing:*

Whether or not they are aware of it, whether or not they are believers, this is from the Christian view fundamental, that doctors are, by their profession, fellow-workers with God. *Professor Courvoisier*

Sickness and healing are acts of grace. *Dr Pouyanne*

The doctor is an instrument of God's patience. *Pastor Alain Perrot*

Medicine is a dispensation of the grace of God.
Dr Schlemmer

I tended him, God healed him. *Ambroise Paré*

Paul Tournier himself describes the task of the doctor as:

Sometimes to heal, often to afford relief, and always to bring consolation.

We now give some prayers for those who are engaged in the different spheres of healing.

O God,
Help me
    to bear the responsibility you have given me
    when I take the lives of others in my hands.
Give me always
    wisdom to see what needs to be done;
    and decision and courage and skill
      to do it.
Help me to remember
    that, when people come to me,
    they are nearly always nervous and frightened,
      and so give me the gift of sympathy,
      so that I may comfort as well as heal.
Help me to remember,
    that, when I heal,
      I do what Jesus did,
      and that you work through me.
This I ask for your love's sake. AMEN

O God,
When people come to me,
　help me always
　to ease the pain
　　and to strengthen the weakness of their bodies,
　　　and to calm the anxieties of their minds.
Help me never to think of them as cases,
　but always as persons.
Help me to be patient,
　when I need to be patient,
and to be stern,
　when I need to be stern.
Help me to remember that,
　when I bring health to the sick and the suffering,
　　the healing work of Jesus
　　is being continued through me,
　　and that I am helping you
　　　to defeat the world's disease and pain.
This I ask for your love's sake. AMEN

O God,
Help me
    to fit myself for the task and the responsibility
      of being a doctor.
Help me to be
  diligent and conscientious in studies.
Help me to learn
    to look on patients not simply
      as bodies which are diseased,
      or minds which are deranged;
  help me never to look on them
      as cases,
      or as specimens of this or that trouble;
  help me
      always to look on them as persons.
Help me to add sympathy,
  which no one can teach me,
  to the skills that I can learn.
Help me to remember
    that ordinary men and women and children
  are always anxious and even afraid
    at the prospect of a visit to the doctor,
  and help me to remember
    that I must comfort and calm
      as well as heal.
Help me always to remember
    that I walk in a great tradition,
    and always to be aware that,
    when I help to heal,
Jesus, the Great Healer, is acting through me.
This I ask for your love's sake. AMEN

O God,
Help me to be a good nurse.
Make me quick and eager in learning,
and wise and efficient in action.
Give me
   patience with people
      who are irritating and demanding and annoying.
Give me
   firmness with people
      who are foolish and stubborn,
         and disobedient and unco-operative.
Give me
   sympathy with people
      who are nervous and anxious and frightened.
Help me to be
   kind when I need to be kind,
   and severe when I need to be severe.
Help me always to remember
   that, when I share in the work of healing,
   I share in the work of Jesus,
      who healed all those who had need of healing.
This I ask for your love's sake. AMEN

O God,
I am often the first person people meet
  when they come to hospital.
Help me to meet them
  with a welcome that is cheerful and kind.
Help me to give people
  the impression of a hospital as a place
    where they really care for people,
      not just as cases, but as persons.
When Jesus was here amongst men, he healed people
  and all who are engaged in healing
    still do his work.
Help me to do my job
  as a real part of the great task of healing,
  and to know that I am sharing the work
    of those who carried people to Jesus,
      so that he might heal them.
This I ask for Jesus' sake. AMEN

O God,
I am usually the first person whom people meet
  when they actually come through the doors of the hospital.
Make me always courteous and always kind,
  and always interested in them.
Help me to remember that
  for nearly everyone who comes to it for the first time
    a hospital is a strange place,
      and they are all nervous and a little afraid
        of what is going to happen to them.
Help me to try to put them at their ease.
Help me to try
  to combine efficiency with kindness,
    and always to remember
    that I am the person
      whose job it is to welcome
      people who are in trouble.
This I ask for Jesus' sake. AMEN

O God,
Most of my work is done behind the scenes,
   and I do not have such direct contact with patients
     as doctors and nurses have.
But help me
   to see people in everything I do.
Help me to remember that,
   no matter what I do,
     it is done to help someone
       who needs help and healing.
So help me
   always to be faithful in my work,
This I ask for Jesus' sake. AMEN

O God,
Give me what I need to make me able
  to do my work well.
Give me
  the patience
    that no failure can discourage;
  the accuracy
    that will save me from all careless and all hurried work;
  the perseverance
    that is undeterred by difficulties or delays.
Help me all the time I am working
  to see, beyond the walls of my laboratory,
    to the people
      whose trouble will be cured,
      and whose pain will be eased,
        if I succeed in what I am trying to do.
So direct my mind,
  and guide my hands,
    that I may search and find.
This I ask for Jesus' sake. AMEN

O God,
Help me to remember the importance of the work
   that I do in this hospital.
The most necessary thing of all in a hospital
   is that it should be clean;
     and it is my job
       to make it and to keep it clean.
Give me pride in my work,
   and help me to do it gladly and cheerfully,
   so that I may bring sunshine and happiness
     into the wards in which I work.
Help me always to remember
   that I and my work
     are essential to the healing of the patients
     in this hospital.
This I ask for Jesus' sake. AMEN

O God,
It is my work
   to bring people who are ill to this hospital.
Help me always to do it
   with speed and yet with safety,
   with efficiency and yet with gentleness.
Help me never to find it a nuisance
   when I am called out
   at an awkward time or to an awkward place.
And help me to bring
   all the comfort and encouragement I can
     to those who are in my care.
This I ask for Jesus' sake. AMEN

O God,
Help me to realise and always to remember
  how big a share I have
  in the helping and the healing
    of the patients in this hospital.
There is nothing more important
  than that they should get
    the right food prepared in the right way.
I hardly ever see the patients
  for whom I prepare the food;
    but in spite of that help me always to be thinking of them
      as persons whom I am helping.
So give me pride
  in preparing food as well as I can,
  and in keeping this kitchen as spotless as I can.
And help me always to remember
  that this hospital could not go on at all
    without my work.
This I ask for Jesus' sake. AMEN

O God,
You have given me a very important place
  in the life and work of this hospital.
It is to me that people come
  with all kinds of problems.
Help me to be efficient,
  but at the same time help me to be kind.
Give me
  patience
    with those who are foolish and helpless
    and disorganised and even ungrateful.
Give me
  sympathy
    with those who are lonely and old,
    with those who are anxious,
      because they have no one to help them
      when they leave the hospital;
    with those who are worried,
      because they know that they will not be strong enough
      for the work that awaits them at home.
Help me to be firm
  with the lazy and the malingerers,
  with those who grumble and complain,
    however much is done for them,
  and with those who will not help themselves.
Help me to be all things to all kinds of people.
Help me
  to see things clearly,
  and to take decisions quickly and firmly.
And help me at all times
  to desire only to help and to comfort.
This I ask for Jesus' sake. AMEN

O God,
All kinds of things have to be done in a hospital
   in order that its healing work may go on efficiently.
   Appointments have to be made;
   records have to be kept;
   letters have to be written and answered;
   stores have to be checked;
   finance has to be looked after.
It is in this part of the work
   that my task lies.
Help me to remember
   that in my own way
      I too am engaged in the work of healing,
      because it could not go on without my work.
Help me to remember that
   behind every record card and letter
      there is a living person with a living need.
So keep me from becoming the kind of administrator
   who is more interested
      in procedures and statistics
      than in persons and people.
Help me always to remember
   that ultimately I am dealing with human beings
      and keep me human.
This I ask for Jesus' sake. AMEN

75 76 77 78 79 10 9 8 7 6 5 4 3 2 1